Wish I would have met Delilah a great dog! [signature] 12/09

ACKNOWLEDGEMENTS

With heartfelt appreciation I thank all the good folks who readily chatted with me while I was meeting their dogs. Hopefully, I've accurately related their comments.

I especially thank my sister, Barbara King and my friends, Sally Bourne and Barbara Hunt, for their editing expertise.

And finally, loving thanks is extended to my dear Tom for his encouragement to me in the journaling of these many dog encounters. "Dog sightings" *together* continues to be such fun!

Dogs I've Met

A journal of dogs and what their owners said about them

Jessie Bailey Crook

authorHOUSE®

AuthorHouse™
1663 Liberty Drive, Suite 200
Bloomington, IN 47403
www.authorhouse.com
Phone: 1-800-839-8640

First published by AuthorHouse 9/14/2009

ISBN: 978-1-4389-0056-8 (sc)

Library of Congress Control Number: 2009906310

*Printed in the United States of America
Bloomington, Indiana*

This book is printed on acid-free paper.

CONTENTS

"We long for an affection altogether ignorant of our faults. Heaven has accorded this to us in the uncritical canine attachment."

George Eliot

INTRODUCTION

Meeting dogs has become a favorite pastime of mine. Whenever I traveled without my three "boys," I enjoyed talking to dogs I'd meet as solace for missing my three. Taking my dogs with me was never an option when I made my annual international study tour with my foreign language middle school students or when I traveled abroad with friends. Cameron, Simba, and Trixster couldn't go with me, so they'd stay home with my husband, Tom. When Tom and I took summer camping trips through the western United States on our motorcycle, our "boys" would stay at our farm in Ohio, being cared for by neighbors and family members.

Whether I traveled abroad or nearer home, I often saw dogs being enjoyed and loved by their owners. I'd feel homesick for my own three and their playful, loving cuddles. So whenever possible, I stopped and talked to a dog, often learning something about it from the owner. In my daily journal I'd jot down the names of the dogs I met and what I learned about them. Writing about the dogs I met while traveling helped to ease my loneliness for my own dogs.

During those joyful years of having three dogs, I enjoyed talking about them to other dog owners, who usually told me their dog's name and often why they were given the name. I sometimes told how our first dog, Cameron, got his name. He was a beagle-ish puppy who followed Cameron, one of my school's sixth graders, to school one morning. Cameron's teacher allowed him to keep the puppy in their classroom until lunchtime. The lunchroom workers wouldn't permit the dog in the lunchroom, so Cameron asked if I'd keep the puppy in my office, claiming he knew the owner and would return the puppy at the end of the school day.

While cuddling the sweet puppy, I remembered that my husband often said we couldn't have a dog because they require too much work and attention. However, he also said if he ever *did* have a dog, it would be a beagle.

After school I drove Cameron around the neighborhood, searching for someone to keep the puppy. Nobody claimed to know its owner, and Cameron's mom wouldn't let him keep it. What was I to do? Of course, name the pup "Cameron" and take him home with me to be our first dog of the three.

My husband was immediately taken with the little guy, who was such a funny, active dog and easily housetrained, as long as anything he might want to eat or chew was kept from him. Cameron Louis settled into our life and was soon indispensable to us. (I added "Louis" because student Cameron studied French at my school, and I liked saying the name "Louis" with the French pronunciation: "loo-*ee*.")

Interestingly enough, two years later when Cameron was in eighth grade, he came to my office with another dog tale. It seemed a man had come to the school playground on two consecutive days asking students if they wanted the big yellow dog he had at the end of a choker collar and rope. Finally, when no students would take the dog, the man left him there, waiting by the building.

"He's a nice dog, so can't you please take him home to be with Cameron?" Cameron begged.

I explained that I didn't think my husband would want another dog. However, Cameron and other students persuaded me to try to help. I went to the playground with them to look at the dog. He was standing near the building with his head hanging down, as if he'd been told to stay there.

When I knelt in front of the shepherd mix and took his head in my hands, he gazed at me with beautiful, dark, soulful eyes. My heart melted as I looked at his trusting face. His wide yellow head made me think of a lion, so I said, "He's a Simba dog!" I told the students if the dog was still there after school I'd consider taking him home with me.

A phone call to my husband, who said to do whatever I thought best, gave me some guidance in deciding what to do about the big yellow dog.

When I went to my car after school that day, Cameron and several other students were waiting there with Simba. They were holding him with a new leash made of a man's silk necktie that a student had in his locker.

"Cameron, I may not want to always call him Simba. What is your middle name?" I asked.

"Leon!" was his answer.

"That's almost like 'lion,'" the students chorused.

So the second dog of our three became Simba Leon.

**Simba Leon and Cameron Louis
Our "Too" Outdoor Dogs**

(If it was <u>too</u> hot, I brought them inside the house. If it was <u>too</u> cold, I brought them inside the house. If it was <u>too</u> rainy or windy, I brought them inside the house.)

Our third dog, Trixster, had been my parents' last dog. He was a stray who came to their farm. Dad named the little male fox terrier Trixie because he'd had a similar dog, a female, many years before.

Trixie was a superior guard dog, who could hear or sense when any vehicle came down the gravel lane toward my parents' farmhouse. He would bark incessantly in his little-dog, high-pitched voice, announcing to my elderly parents that a visitor was approaching. Dad would motion behind his chair and say, "Into your bomb shelter, Trixie!" and the little dog would run behind Dad's recliner and lay down. From there Trixie would emit an occasional low growl to remind visitors that he was still on duty.

As my parents became more aged and infirm, Trixie was a loyal comfort and joy to them. He would lie on the floor beside Mom's side of the bed every minute she was in the bed, day or night. After Mom's death, Trixie became Dad's constant security guard, sleeping at the foot of his bed. Dad often voiced his concern to me about what would happen to Trixie after he was gone. Because I was the one in our large family who bathed Trixie, brushed him, and generally cuddled him whenever I visited, I was pleased to promise Dad that I would take Trixie to live at our house. My husband, however, told me in private, "I don't want that yipping dog to come live with us!"

When the time came for me to bring Trixie home, my husband quickly accepted him, mainly because Trixie ceased barking at our house! We figured Trixster must have decided he didn't need to guard us, so he retired from his security guard duties! Because he was a male, we began calling him Trixster, or Trix, a more masculine name. In fact, when he came to live at our farm he became such a sweet, well-behaved dog we often referred to him as "The Prince of Sunnyfield Farm."

Trixster, the Prince of Sunnyfield Farm

Now, since the death of Trixster due to old age, the disappearance of Cameron when he didn't return from a hunt at our farm, and most recently the cancer-related euthanasia of Simba, I've become a Dog Person With No Dog.

Since we've both retired from teaching, Tom and I live in a small condo most of the year and along with frequent travels it's difficult for us to have a dog right now. My therapy and regular joy is meeting dogs, regardless of whether I encounter them walking with their people in my neighborhood, at rest areas along the highway during our trips between Ohio and Florida, or in my domestic and international travels. Because most dog people readily talk about their dogs, it's my pleasure to spend a few minutes whenever possible talking to a dog and loving it like it's my own.

My standard opening to the dog is, "Aren't you a darling … sweetheart, champion, baby,"—whatever endearment comes to mind. I follow that with a question to the owner: "What's your dog's name?" Most owners are thrilled at the attention shown their beloved pets. Usually a wellspring of stories and explanations pours forth from the owners about their dog's name, what life is like with their dog, and the pup's idiosyncrasies.

This book is a compilation of notes from my journals about brief meetings with dogs and their owners during my daily walks and in my travels near and far. Since the death of our last dog, Simba, I've become more purposeful in my collection of dog names and their owners' comments about them. As everyone who has had to euthanize a dear pet knows, my grief from the loss of Simba was excruciating. Meetings with other dogs have helped me through the mourning stages of living without him. This book recalls those many warm, sweet times when I've petted and massaged the *Dogs I've Met*.

WYOMING

During a summer camping trip with my husband on our motorcycle, we stopped in the small towns of Cody, Dubois, and Jeffery, where I enjoyed meeting the following memorable dogs:

Zuni, a shepherd mix, wore a collar, tags, and a red bandana, which made him an appropriately dressed dog in Cody, a rodeo town. Zuni lived at the local mercantile, where he had free rein. He eagerly played with a tennis ball and with any customer who couldn't resist his good-natured interest.

Tarquas was a six-month-old black and brown Alaskan malamute. His name came from a favorite video game character. He was an obedient, sweet-natured dog who stayed in the open bed of his owner's pickup truck while his master went inside the nearby café. His owner predicted that Tarquas would grow to be 190 pounds, so he was delighted that Tarquas was a good dog, exclaiming to me, "Who wants a *large* disobedient dog?"

Samantha (Sammy), a yellow-coated mix, was the newest member of a family of eight dogs living at a small roadside diner. She had been hit by a truck on the nearby highway the year before. She was rescued and had been a happy member of the diner family ever since. Each dog had his or her picture displayed on a bulletin board by the front door. It was obvious that the diner's patrons were dog lovers because after I briefly petted and talked to her, Sammy followed me inside, where she received more greetings and pets from several of the folks dining there. The dogs had good sleeping accommodations in individual doghouses behind the diner.

Sarah Anne (Annie) was a four-year-old black poodle whom I met while she was being walked by her elderly mistress at a campground. "What a darling little dog!" was my greeting. I then learned that Annie was the lady's second poodle. For fifteen years she'd had a white poodle who, six months earlier, died of congestive heart failure. While I was petting Annie, the dear lady told me, "Annie is the perfect dog for me. I also suffer from congestive heart failure, so I wanted an older dog that wouldn't outlive me too long."

KYOTO, JAPAN

While leading an academic study tour to Japan with Japanese language students from my middle school, I saw very few dogs. However, I was pleased to get the chance to meet one sweet dog there and felt a bit of comfort while missing my own.

Winston was a low-slung, brown West Highland terrier who was being walked on a leash near the train station. The little dog exhibited all the traits of a well-trained, obedient pet as he strutted along. He stopped and sat when his owner stopped at the crosswalk. His owner didn't speak English, and I don't speak Japanese, but through the universal sign language of pointing to myself and stating my name, I determined that the well-behaved dog's name was Winston.

Wouldn't it be interesting to know how the little Japanese dog got the name "Winston?" Because the dog's owner was an elderly lady, I speculated that she may have heard that name from world news of Winston Churchill and liked the sound of it. Or maybe she had an association with the American cigarettes by that name? I'll never know.

ATHENS, GREECE

While traveling in Greece with my husband and a group of friends, I saw a multitude of dogs. Most of them were strays living among the many ruins we visited and being fed a diet of snacks from soft-hearted tourists. The dogs also ate from the trash cans filled with discarded food and drinks. At the Acropolis, no less than fifteen dogs were lying about in the shade, seemingly content living on their own. There were shepherds, boxers, schnauzers, and many mutts of mixed lineage. Because the dogs were dusty and sometimes even mangy looking, I wasn't surprised that no one was petting or talking to them.

One dog caught my attention, however. He was lying in the shade, snoring contentedly. He had a familiar yellow coat, broad head, and blond "sidelights" on his shoulders. I sat on a bench nearby and tearfully watched him, missing my Simba, whom he so strongly resembled.

Our guide explained that Athens has a problem with so many stray dogs, especially at the Acropolis, where they come every day for their "meals." The campaign to encourage the spaying or neutering and leashing of all household dogs didn't seem to be making an impact on the number of stray dogs wandering the streets. When cleaning up after the dogs became too big of a job, city officials rounded up the dogs and euthanized them. With so many dogs there on the day we visited, we were cautioned to "watch your step."

Of the many dogs I saw in Athens, I only met three: *Shadow, Wolfie, and Hectorus* were beautiful, lushly coated huskies playing off-leash in a small park near our Divani Caravel hotel.

The dogs' owner ignored the posted signs stating that dogs must be leashed. He was very attentive to them, however, tossing a ball and calling their names to keep them close. I walked near the owner, who saw me admiring his happy dogs. I learned that Shadow, with his distinctive characteristic of one dark eye and one blue eye, was the father of brothers Wolfie and Hectorus. "These three are my family," their owner declared to me.

While Wolfie and Hectorus romped and rolled with each other, the more sedate Shadow chased the ball and repeatedly returned it to their owner. The man told me the park is the only place near his home where he can bring the dogs for exercise. I noted that he did clean up after them, a practice that he said most dog owners in Athens ignore.

I-75 BETWEEN OHIO AND FLORIDA

Since we've retired, Tom and I make road trips between our home in Ohio and our small condo in Florida. During the two-day trip, we stop often at service stations and rest areas to stretch our legs and for me to meet dogs! Most of the rest areas have shady, grassy pet-walking space. It seems that many people have no problem traveling with their dogs because we see them all along the way. At each stop, I look forward to discovering what dogs I'll see and hopefully get to meet. My travel journal includes the following dogs I've met at stops along Interstate 75:

Sophie was sitting in the shade at a picnic stop with her owners. From her short-haired brindle coat and stiff-legged stance I guessed she was a basenji.

"Have you seen the movie *Good-bye, My Lady?*" they asked me. "Well, that movie is about a basenji, just like

Sophie." They went on to explain that she was seven years old and didn't bark, but when she was a puppy, she would sometimes make a moaning sound, which is common with basenji pups. "If you're looking for a dog, going barkless is the way to go!" the owner exclaimed.

It was such a pleasure to pet and talk to Sophie, who welcomed my attention as she settled down next to her bowl of water. What a well-tended, sweet little girl dog.

Marina was one of the largest dogs I've met. She was an above-average sized, blond and brown St. Bernard who was waiting by her owner's van at a highway rest area. With her thick, stocky legs and *large* paws she was a lot of dog to pet. I guessed her weight to be about 175 pounds.

"We named her Marina, which is Russian for 'of the sea,' because we were living on a boat when we got her as a puppy," her owner said. "She used to be so aggressive with other dogs, but now (she) lets them crawl all over her. She especially likes the many very small dogs that live in our neighborhood.

"Look at the steps I made for her to walk up so she can get in and out of our van." Marina's owner had a carpeted set of three steps.

Just then, Marina looked down the sidewalk and saw her other owner returning from the restroom. "Awoo, awoo, awoo!" she called loudly. Other travelers in the vicinity laughed to see the joyful reunion of Marina and her owner as they reunited after being away from each other for only a few minutes.

I commented to Marina's owners that one of the reasons we love our dogs so much is because of that constant "glad to see you" welcome they always give. They readily agreed as Marina climbed up her steps and into the van.

Sparky was a stocky-built, black and white Jack Russell terrier who, his owner said, resembles a Champion spark plug. Seeing his one eye circled in black, I replied that he could also model as Nipper, the RCA Victor dog. His mistress, a lady of small stature, told me that Sparky's strong strut made it feel like he was pulling her rather than her walking him on his leash. His master told me that Sparky loved everyone and was much more settled and well-behaved than most Jack Russells.

"One of his favorite tricks is to lure other dogs close with an apparent welcoming wag and wiggle," Sparky's mistress said. "Then when they come close, he backs into my legs and growls aggressively. Needless to say, other dogs don't come near me." Just then Sparky demonstrated that very stunt with a beautiful yellow Lab who was walking nearby! The Lab, with great aplomb, walked away totally undisturbed!

Tanner and *Digger* were two other Jack Russell terriers I met at another rest area the same day. I learned that they had traveled with their truck-driver owner for the last seven years. He said to me, "I have to keep Tanner leashed because he loves to dash around away from me, but Digger stays right at my side when I walk them at rest areas. Digger never jumps up on folks until he thinks Tanner is getting too much attention."

I enjoyed petting and massaging these two precious companions, not minding a bit when they put their front legs on my lap as I knelt to talk to them.

"These two are my favorites of the four dogs I own. I have an Irish setter and Lab who stay home with my wife. Tanner and Digger are the best companions on the road ... real traveling dogs!" he told me. I'm sure he's happy that it's his two *smallest* dogs who are the travelers.

Even though I'd handy-wiped my hands after meeting them, I was pleased to notice I carried away more than just the memory of Tanner and Digger. Their little Jack Russell paw prints were on the front of my jeans!

Jumanji, a black, tan, and white shaggy dog, was waddling for a drink of water with his owner at a highway rest area. As I paused to look at the dog, his owner, who was traveling alone and seemed to want to talk to someone, related the following information: "Jumanji is eleven years old. I got him when that movie first came out, and I liked the name. I don't know what it means.

"He's my dog but has been living with my parents for the past three years. My mom gives him too many treats every day. That's why he's so overweight. I've just spent over three hundred dollars in vet bills for antibiotics to get rid of the skin condition that causes the hair to come off his tail. So far it's not helping him.

"He doesn't like this move we're making to my place. I'll get him on a better diet."

I briefly mentioned the benefits of regular exercise along with a fit-and-trim diet for dogs. Meanwhile, Jumanji was eating a donut! I resisted the urge to comment further and called, "Good luck to you and your good dog!" as I walked on.

Leah was a three-year-old black Lab. "She goes everywhere with us!" her owners said as I paused to admire her during an early morning stop. The elderly couple who owned Leah were walking her in the pet area. "She is such a good dog for us because she's not too lively for us to control."

I thought it seemed that Leah was actually walking her owners as she carefully moved along the sidewalk by their side, almost like a trained companion dog. I mentioned that thought to them, and the lady said, "She was one year old when we got her, and she very quickly settled down, almost like she knew the kind of dog she needed to be." Many dogs do become perfect pets as they sense their owners' needs.

Sally had a thin leash wrapped around her muzzle. "This muzzle isn't because she bites. It's a peace lead and comforts her on this, her first road trip. She's doing really well," explained her owner, a young man traveling alone, as he cuddled the little Jack Russell terrier in his arms. I told him I'd met several Jack Russells at other rest areas and thought they must be really good traveling dogs. Their small-to-medium size makes them good for car trips, but mostly I believe any dog will adjust to going where his or her owner goes because dogs so want to be with us.

Scooby, a beagle–cocker spaniel mix, was sitting in a pickup truck while her owner was pumping gas at a service station where we stopped. I spoke to the little girl dog as I walked near. "What a darling little dog you are!" Her owner laughed as he told me the following about her: "Scooby loves to travel. I've taken her with me from Pennsylvania to Colorado, and now we're on the way to Florida. She has her own water-cooler jug. I like to spoil her. I get her a seventy-five dollar spa treatment once a month."

She was beautifully groomed and obviously very comfortable and confident with me, a stranger, petting her through the open truck window. Even though the spa expenditure the man reported seemed excessive to me, I know many owners spare no expense in caring for and even pampering their dogs.

I remembered bathing our three rough-and-tumble dogs with the hose outside in the summer and in our shower in the winter. In fact, we used a dog groomer only once, when Simba got "skunked" and we had to have his coat treated so we could bring him back into the house. I'm sure the elegant Scooby will never be in a situation where she'll be "skunked."

Tipper was a small, shaggy, black and tan mix. He was walking his owner in a condo community just off I-75 where my husband and I were stopping to golf. Tipper sat like a champion while we asked directions. "He's a good boy, six years old," the owner said. Tipper wagged his tail as he lovingly looked up at his owner. "He understands everything I say to him!" It certainly seemed that Tipper was listening intently, but he made no replies.

Bruiser was a miniature Doberman I met at a service station. The owner explained that he'd been a stray who came to their place. The little boy and girl in the pickup truck with Bruiser shyly smiled as I petted him. "He's really good with the kids, and they love him," the owner told me.

That was one of the many dogs I met whose name didn't seem to fit their personality. I didn't learn how such a sweet, docile dog got the name *Bruiser*.

Max and **Belle** were being walked by their owner at a highway rest area. They were two distinctly different dogs, but it was obvious they were devoted to each other. Max was twice the size of Belle. With his all-black coat and Labrador size, he towered over Belle. She, however, leaned into him as they ran, with her blond Sheltie coat and tail waving in the wind.

The lady who owns them told me, "They are two strays that we found within two weeks of each other. Immediately they became best buddies and are really good dogs to have around. They behave very well in the house, and our kids think they are just two more siblings."

Bailey was a black border collie I met at a highway rest area. It was late at night, and her mistress was walking her in the dog run near the restrooms. "I feel so safe traveling at night with Bailey. She will let you pet her and talk to her but would bark viciously if she thought I was in danger. She is my best friend and such fun to have with me at home and in my car."

Mandy was another medium-sized border collie with a silky black coat. Her owner told me that Mandy had severe hip-displacement problems, and her vet suggested surgery. Mandy was eight years old, and even though that is young to have hip problems, the owner said she can't put Mandy through the trauma of surgery or herself through the expense.

"So I give her an aspirin a day, and that helps her move easier. She loves to travel with me. I work several flea markets up and down the East Coast. Mandy is a good companion for me. She's my security guard!" (I've seen many dogs with their owners at "flea" markets, so I didn't make any comment about dogs and fleas!)

Peewee was a Boston terrier whom I met at another interstate rest area. His trucker master shared the following with me: "Peewee was born on my birthday fourteen months ago. He's the smartest dog you'll ever meet. Look at the way he's letting you pet him. He can be gentle and well-behaved. But when he's in the truck nobody can even get close without him going into a barking, growling rage! My wife worries that if I'd get sick or have a problem and need help, nobody could come help me because Peewee wouldn't let them! But he's the best dog for me."

Keetna was a six-month-old Alaskan malamute with beautiful black and white markings and turquoise eyes. She was leaping at cars and then at me as I walked toward her and her owner.

"May I visit your wonderful dog?" I called.

"Do you want to take her home with you?" was the reply. "She's very friendly but is too much for us. Even after two series of obedience classes, we can't manage her. We even spent an hour with a 'dog-whisperer' trainer, and she still leaps and lunges when I try to walk her on the leash. She is such a sweet dog, but too active for us. We're too old for this!

"She's our third malamute, but the others were so easy to care for. We named her Keetna from a beautiful place we've visited in Alaska, Talkeetna."

I encouraged the owner to stick with the training for herself and her husband because Keetna was still young and, as they learned how to be with her, she probably would become as well behaved as their previous dogs.

When I shared this encounter with Tom after we were back on the road, he said, "I'm glad you didn't bring that big dog with you to the car. Where would she sit?"

He was right because we usually have the car packed pretty full when we make our drives between Florida and Ohio with many things I want to have with me in both homes. So, no room for a dog right now.

Bonnie and **Clyde** were sitting in their owner's SUV at an interstate service station/restaurant.

"What sweet-faced hounds," I called to their mistress. "They look like the hunting dogs my father owned when I was a girl."

"They're beagle/Walker coon hounds," she explained. "Bonnie is the taller one. Clyde was the runt of the litter. I'm going inside to buy them a roast beef sandwich for their dinner."

While she was inside I talked to Bonnie and Clyde through the slightly opened car windows. "You're blue ribbon dogs and I know you must be great hunters," I told them.

Their mistress returned and while she was feeding them each a sandwich she told me, "This is their once-a-week-treat. I think they know when it's time for their sandwich run. They become very animated when we pull into this parking lot."

"What do they usually eat?" I asked.

"They actually have a very strict diet of nutritious Iams dog food," she explained. "Occasionally I give them Milk

Bone treats that seem to help keep their teeth clean and white."

I complimented her on her pups' apparent fitness with their sleek coats and calm, happy demeanors. It was a pleasure to meet Bonnie and Clyde and be reminded of great times hunting with my dad and his Redbone, Walker, and Blue Tick hounds.

Bud Weiner, a low-slung dachshund, was being walked without a leash in the pet park at a highway rest area.

"What a well-trained little dog! He certainly stays close to you," I called to his mistress.

"I'd usually have him on a leash but I left it in our motor home that my husband is driving. I thought he was right behind me on the highway. Bud needed to be walked so here I am without his leash. Bud does stay close to me with very few verbal reminders."

"He's a beautiful dog," I told her, as I admired his shiny coat with brown, blond and red markings down his sides and on his silky tail.

"Bud is two years old. When we first got him we tried for several weeks to decide on a name. We even searched names on the internet. During the entire time we were calling him *Bud*, so the name stuck. Friends laughingly called him *Budweiser*, but we wanted something more high-class. We decided "Bud Weiner" was better suited to his breed and regal character."

I remember him as one of the most obedient and well-trained dogs I met.

DOGS I KNOW

Buddy
Naples, Florida

"There is only one smartest dog in the world and every boy has it."   *Unknown*

Bailey
Columbia, South Carolina

"A dog wags his tail with his heart."   *Martin Buxbaum*

Putter
Avon, Ohio

"J'embrasse mon chien sur la bouche!"
(I kiss my dog on the mouth!)   *Unknown*

Quincy
Westerville, Ohio

"Dogs are not our whole life, but they make our
lives whole."   *Roger Caras*

NAPLES, FLORIDA

My husband and I live in a small condo on a golf course in Naples, Florida, several months of the year. Besides golfing, we also enjoy walks on the many beaches in the area, as well as bicycling and walking in our neighborhood and nearby communities and parks. We dine out often with friends, and I'm fond of visiting the many beautiful shops of all kinds in the area. In other words, we are out and about most of the months we spend in southwest Florida. I'm happy to report that there are dogs everywhere, and my journal becomes full of notes about my encounters. The following are dogs I've met in and around Naples:

"**Sammy** is his name, but we call him many things: Samsonite, Samsung, our little Sweetie Pie!" his owners explained about their small, old Chihuahua outside Nonna Maria's Italian restaurant. As my husband and I were entering to dine with friends, Sammy's family, a young woman and her mother, father and aunt, were leaving the restaurant. The young woman, who was carrying Sammy in her arms, commented that Nonna Maria's was one of Sammy's favorite restaurants.

"We like to be seated in the back lanai area where Sammy can sit on my lap, tasting an occasional bite, and nobody minds him being there."

As we've gotten to know Naples, we find one of the things that make it beautiful, besides its tropical climate, is that many restaurants and shops welcome small dogs.

Tama is a rescued greyhound whom I met while walking in our neighborhood. I stopped to pet her and told her owner that I'd never met a greyhound. I said Tama seemed to be such a docile, sweet girl.

The lady explained that Tama had come to her from several months in foster care where she was brought back to health after a hard life as a track dog. During that time, Tama had several strokes and nearly died after a surgery to remove two of her toes. The toe surgery had been necessary because her toes wouldn't heal, a common condition with greyhounds who've spent years racing. The owner then went on to describe her own double knee replacement surgery and how Tama limped around the house comforting her when she'd had Tama only two weeks. "Tama is such a loving, loyal dog. She is a constantly good-natured companion."

Tama's owner said she'd recommend greyhound rescue to anyone looking for a good dog and that they're especially great with children.

Doby is a small, light brown dachshund who came down the sidewalk with his owner while I was petting Tama. He lives near Tama, and they are great friends. When they met on the sidewalk, even though they are entirely mismatched in size, they ran to each other, sniffed, romped, and played like two children.

"These two are great friends who meet every day if we're both walking our dogs at the same time," Doby's owner told me.

I've since seen these two on a driveway of another condo on our street. A group of four or five ladies and a couple of men meet almost every day around five o'clock for what they call "Yappy Hour." Owners come with their beverages in hand and dogs on leashes, and they stand or sit around chatting while the dogs visit. The dogs are all medium to small sized and are well behaved with each other.

Sometimes I'm walking or riding my bicycle at that time and often call out, "I wish I had a dog. I'd come join you!" Maybe someday!

NOTE: With all the traveling Tom and I do, he feels it would not be good to have a dog right now. I jokingly accuse him of trying to clip my wings by making me rethink my desire to do international traveling every year. We both enjoy our many friends who come with their dogs to visit us at our farm in Ohio and at our condo in Florida. I'm hoping we'll soon reconsider the stipulation that only when I'm ready to stay put in one place can we have a dog (or two) again.

Cosmo was a two-year-old, white, black and tan shih tzu whom her owner was carrying into Lowe's. I stopped to admire Cosmo, saying she looked like a friend's dear dog. The owner said, "She's our second shih tzu. We had to put our other one, Francis, to sleep last year. Cosmo is such a good dog too."

Her owner explained that because of the heat in Naples, they never leave Cosmo in the car when they're shopping. "She loves to go with us wherever we go. Lowe's and no other store has ever objected when we carry Cosmo while shopping." She did admit that they *never* take her into grocery stores.

Sarah and *Keegan* were greyhound show dogs whom I learned about from their owner who was seated near us at a breakfast diner. He related to Tom and me that he was traveling with his dogs who were with his wife at the nearby hotel.

"They've won many Best of Show and second-place awards all over the country. We enjoy taking them to dog shows where we've made many friends from all over the country. We love them so much it doesn't matter if they're actually winners or not," their owner explained. "They are true champions to my wife and me!"

Jessica was a seemingly very old Chihuahua whose owners I didn't meet. She was gated in a small bathroom of a condo that was being shown by Realtors at an open house near our neighborhood. A friend and I stopped in while bike riding, curious to see what the nearby condos were like.

Jessica was frightened and shivering violently because strangers were in her house. I talked to her, and after letting her smell my hand, I petted her for a few minutes, but she continued to tremble. The Realtor on site had moved on to another condo open house nearby, and I didn't wait around to learn more about Jessica. However, I did phone the Realtor's office and explained Jessica's trauma. I suggested that, if possible, the owners take her out when their condo is being shown.

Niko, a tan and white schnauzer, was being carried in the arms of his owner during sunset on Vanderbilt Beach. The young woman holding Niko related the following to me as I petted him: "We come here often for the sunset, and Niko always loves it. He's three years old, and today is his birthday! That's why we brought him to the beach. He loves it here!"

What a beautiful place to celebrate a special day, as the pink, mauve, and turquoise colors of that lovely spot glowed in Niko's eyes. Happy birthday, happy dog!

Petey was a sixteen-year-old, black, shiny-coated shepherd mix whom I met while he was being walked near our condo. "What a sweet old friend!" was my first comment to his owner.

With the soulful eyes of a most-loyal dog, Petey "doesn't know a stranger. He'd go home with the last person who patted his head," his owner said. Petey pressed into my leg as I petted his graying face and coat. He was letting me know he could take all the massages and pats I had for him.

Merlot was a striking apricot and white poodle who Tom and I met while visiting a condo with our realtor. Merlot's mistress welcomed us at the door and told us to not be afraid of Merlot because he likes people. I asked how he got his "delicious" name.

"I named him after the wine I was enjoying at the time," she explained. "He's a smart dog with great time and place perception. He always lets me know when it's supper time or if he thinks it's time for a walk. Also, he seems to know when he's going to the vet or the boarding kennel. Merlot doesn't like either place so he cries all the way in the car. However, he never cries on the way home. As I said, he likes people but especially likes babies."

"He's such a sweet, small baby himself," I told her as I petted that handsome poodle.

An old **"beagle-ish"** dog came to our door and inside our lanai where I gave him a drink of cold water. He wouldn't let me check his tags, shying away whenever I tried to hold him. Then, with a longing look out of his old eyes, he nudged the screen, letting me know that he wanted to continue on his walk. I watched him visit at each door up the street.

I was relieved to later see him in the garage at a home down the street with his owner. He'd simply been out on a solo walk in the neighborhood and then returned to his family who, I later learned, were renting a vacation home.

Zoe was a sleek-coated, light tan pit bull–shepherd mix whom I met on an early morning walk in our neighborhood. She jumped playfully like any eight-month-old pup. Her loving owners described her as "the very good replacement for the dog we'd had for twelve years.

"Zoe found us at the local shelter, and she instantly bonded with us. She was so happy we'd found her and let us know by clinging to us in the car all the way home."

The owners, a young couple, explained that Zoe quickly filled the void left by their previous dog because her antics and good nature are similar.

Jackson lived near the golf course and enjoyed romping and playing keep-away with a football. His loving owners described their golden brown, sweet-faced pit bull as "usually very shy with strangers. What a surprise that he's so friendly with you!" I explained that kids and dogs almost always love Aunt Jessie.

Jackson's owners told me that he needed a lot of exercise and encouraged me to stop by whenever I wanted to play with him. As I massaged Jackson and he looked at me out of his Simba-like eyes, with their dark rims and loving loyalty, I got weepy remembering my own dear dog.

To explain my tears, I told Jackson's owners how his coat color and loyal eyes reminded me of Simba, the dog I'd enjoyed having for nine years before his death from cancer.

"We certainly understand your pain. Jackson is our second dog, and just thinking about him dying breaks our hearts."

We then discussed how dogs don't live long enough and their time with us is always too short. Jackson's owners told me that they understood the lingering sorrow that comes from the loss of a dog. Their previous dog had died about two years ago. My Simba's death had been a year and a half before. Good dogs are remembered, missed, and loved forever.

Unnamed dog was a medium-sized, gray wire-haired cutie sitting in his owner's pickup truck at a service station. Besides the fact it was another dog for me to possibly meet and jot into my journal, this dog grabbed my attention because he looked like a little woodchuck sitting behind the steering wheel, waiting for his owner to "Fill 'er up, Mister!"

The dog's owner gave me a friendly grin when he saw me walking slowly past, smiling at his dog. I was about to ask the dog's name when, in a very unfriendly fashion, the dog jumped from the steering wheel to the closed window and growled only two words: "Grrrr, grrr!" I continued smiling as I walked by. The little dog was taking his guard duty seriously. Good dog! (Although I didn't actually meet this little guy, my "woodchuck" vision of him found its way into my dog journal.)

Cinnamon and **Bailey** were two girl dogs. Cinnamon, a reddish brown setter, and Bailey, a black Lab, could often be seen lying outside their house on the lawn bordering our community golf course.

They were not leashed, which goes against Naples's leash law. It seemed unnecessary for these two beauties to be leashed. Their owner was always sitting on the ground beside them brushing their coats. What dog would run away from that welcome treatment?

Often when golfing past, I softly called their names just to see their heads come up and their tails wag. Their owner called out their names to me the first time I noticed them there, but with a small lake between us, I've not been able to go to them for a close meeting. However, the two quiet, beautiful dogs always calmly watch me and the antics of any golfers on the nearby eleventh green.

Echo, Dakota, and **Cajun** were waiting patiently for their owner as she pumped gas at a service station in Naples where Tom and I purchased our morning newspaper.

"Aren't you lucky to have three such nice dogs? What are their names?" I greeted her.

"Echo and Dakota are the large ones, both Lab mixes, and Cajun is the little pit bull. I'm making the move to Colorado from Florida for a job transfer. These three are my best friends, so they have to go with me," she explained. Her three friends leaned out the window, looking as if they were totally enjoying the adventure.

"What a fun time you'll have with these good friends!" I told her as we walked past.

I regret that I didn't stop to hear the origin of their names. I probably missed a memorable story!

Tyke was a two-month-old yellow Lab whom I didn't meet but heard about during a golf outing. Including Tyke in my journal and in this writing seemed appropriate because of the lengthy conversation during which I began to feel like I *had* met him.

Chad, my cart partner, told me he and his fiancé were living the American dream. They had good jobs, a new house, and had just got their dog. "Tyke has become like our child, our little tyke. We play with him every minute we can. He already likes only the best puppy food, Iams. Our vet recommended Iams or Science Diet, but Tyke went for the Iams right off."

I told him that several friends of mine also only use Iams for their dogs. For several golf holes we discussed the benefits of different dog foods.

I explained that we fed our Trixster Mighty Dog Senior, Fit and Trim, because when he came to us from my father, he was many pounds overweight. My dad fed Trix the farmers' diet that he was accustomed to: bacon, fried eggs, gravy, etc. In fact, Dad liked to joke, "Trix is so fat a person could play solitaire on his back!" When Trixster came to live with Tom and me, the fit-and-trim program, with regular exercise, helped him reach a healthier twelve pounds in just a few months.

Chad told me that Tyke may grow to be 120 pounds. "We want our soon-to-be-big dog to be well behaved. We've already started puppy obedience classes with him."

I agreed that for any size dog and his or her owner, obedience classes are important if they don't want their "American dream" to become a nightmare.

Amy was a medium-sized, light brown and blond shepherd–Shiba Inu mix who was being walked by a nanny pushing a baby in a pram. I was walking to the market for our Naples morning newspaper when I stopped to talk to the nanny.

"What a beautiful little dog! She looks like a small fox with that lush tail curled over her back!" was my introductory comment.

"Amy is such a good dog and very affectionate. She belongs to my employers, but I love her and the baby like they're my own. I'm very happy to work for a family with such a nice dog as Amy," the nanny explained.

I noted that Amy sat very alertly but noticed every vehicle or bicyclist who passed by.

"Amy is a shelter dog, and when I first began walking her, she would bark, leap, and lunge at anyone or thing that passed by. We're using the bark collar on her until she learns to not bark at every sound. It always wakes the baby."

The nanny continued by saying she thinks Amy just wants everyone to notice her. "She likes it that you stopped to pet her; that's why she sits so nicely. She is becoming such a good dog, and now only barks at large, loud trucks that pass by."

I told the nanny that her employers were fortunate to find someone like her who loved their child *and* their dog.

NOTE: As I continued my walk, I smiled thinking how my husband and many friends would laugh that I knew more about Amy, the dog, than I did the baby sleeping in the pram (although I did learn his name and that he loves having Amy nearby). Tom and I are aunt and uncle to many nieces and nephews in both of our families. We love them all dearly and have always felt blessed to be an aunt and uncle, watching and helping our nieces and nephews grow up. We've not missed being parents. As classroom teachers, we've been happy to expend our parenting instincts on our students. Although Tom isn't quite as passionate about dogs as I am, he loved and took good care of our dogs when we had them. He understands the joy dogs give me and considers me meeting dogs to be a worthwhile hobby. He often points out dogs I might miss seeing as we travel, and he encourages my journaling of dog meetings. Many of our friends are also great dog lovers and understand how, because I grew up on a family farm that included many hunting dogs, I can appreciate all types of dogs.

Bamm Bamm was a small white and tan Pekingese-Chihuahua mix with large eyes and tall ears. I met her on another early morning walk for the newspaper in Naples. "Here's a precious little beauty!" was my first comment when I saw her walking toward me on the sidewalk.

Her owner stopped for me to meet Bamm Bamm and said, "We were going to name her Thor, but we didn't think that suited her appearance. However, her personality and attitude are sometimes very Thor-like. She barks at everyone.

"Of course, as you can see, she then wiggles all over, licking them with joy! We named her Bamm Bamm from Pebbles and Bamm-Bamm in the *Flintstones*." I think the name fit her feminine appearance and her assertive personality.

Lucky was a beautiful, small tan Italian greyhound. When I first met him early one morning walking with his owner in our Naples neighborhood, I was told, "His name is Lucky, and he's *lucky* to be alive after barking all night and keeping me awake!"

A few months later I saw him again and learned this from the young woman who owned him: "He's the first dog I've had who is all mine and not my parents' or family's dog. I don't know how I could love him more. He is so sweet and special." Good dog, good owner!

Buddy the Beagle's owners were walking him near our golf course in Naples when we first met. I was especially drawn to Buddy because he looked almost exactly like my own beagle-ish Cameron, who'd been gone for several years by then.

Buddy's owners, our nearby neighbors, told me they had purchased him from a breeder in Miami at a purebred beagle price. However, they discovered too late that he was actually a mix. It was too late because they love him too much to care whether he is or isn't purebred!

Buddy's previous life in Miami must have been a violent one. Several weeks after buying him from the unscrupulous breeder, Buddy's owners noticed a seeping cyst on his thigh. They treated it with antibiotics, and Buddy licked it often, as dogs tend to do to promote self-healing. Over several weeks, the cyst healed and then reappeared. Finally a small-caliber bullet oozed out! Thankfully, soon after that the wound totally healed.

Each person in the family of four has worked hard to help Buddy acclimate to his new home. For the first few days, he had several problem incidents. Once, when he was first left alone, he chewed and scratched his way out of his wire crate and proceeded to tear up the house by jumping and running over tables and the kitchen counters. Of course, every item on each surface crashed to the floor. Another incident involved Buddy chewing up a pincushion full of straight pins and scattering them over the floor before anyone noticed what he was doing.

Now after a few months of training and attention, Buddy the Beagle is a happy, well-behaved, and much-loved dog in his new life

Ned was a brown, sleek-coated, frisky hound puppy being walked for one of his first times on a leash. I was riding my bicycle in Naples when I first saw Ned. He looked very much like the hunting hounds my father raised when I was a child.

"What a fine-looking hound!" I called out as I stopped to meet him. "Is he a hunting dog?" I asked.

"I'm actually not Ned's owner. I'm his neighbor giving his owners a break. As you can see, it is exhausting trying to walk Ned. We jokingly say it takes a whole village to raise Ned!"

A few weeks later I saw Ned again, much taller already and walking much better on the leash, but far out in front of his owners. When I stopped to pet Ned, the young couple who owns him told me he is their first dog. I wished them the best of luck as they learned to harness and direct the energy of their sweet dog.

Zane lived in a beautiful house in Naples with his owners, a middle-aged married couple, and Bud, the other dog in the family whom I didn't meet.

Zane was a handsome, strongly built boxer–American Staffordshire terrier mix. His owner explained that Zane, a recent addition to their family, walked on the leash much better when the easy-going Bud stayed inside.

Zane's most striking feature was his black spotted ears. His owner related the following: "Those ears indicate there was a Dalmatian in there somewhere in 'Insane Zane's' lineage. Our daughter and her roommate found him in an alley. They spent several days feeding him outside and continued visiting him after he was placed in the animal shelter.

"Zane was a dead dog walking, just hours from being culled to make space at the shelter, when the girls took him to their apartment. Soon he was dropped off at our house, and that's where he's been since.

"I'm disappointed that my daughter hasn't taken responsibility for Zane. He is so happy to see her when she visits and obviously looks to her as his true master. My mother-in-law said we should be happy she's brought home a four-legged child for us to raise, rather than a two-legged one!"

Zane quietly sat watching cars and neighbors passing in the street, seeming to enjoy hearing his biography. When the little dog across the street came outside, Zane went into his "insane" mode, jumping, flipping, and spinning on his leash like a gymnastics medalist.

Andre and Ivy were a brother and sister duo I met while riding my bicycle in a beautiful golf course community. Their owners, two couples standing nearby, told me they were letting their Bichon Frises have a "play date." The two fluffy, white-coated pups rolled and tumbled with each other while I learned the following from their owners.

"We're neighbors, just around the corner from each other and happened to hear of these two being available from a breeder in Clearwater. We'd not had a dog for years and decided to each get one so we'd both always have someone to dog-sit when needed."

"Andre keeps us laughing every day. It is so funny watching his ears perk up when we mention Ivy's name. He found some bubble gum in the grass recently and we had to scrape it off of his nose!"

"Ivy seems to be the alpha dog of the pair...look how she topples him over, but he loves it and always goes in for more!"

"What great exercise they give each other!" I observed.

"They each get several walks a day so we're all getting our exercise too!"

Mia was a West Highland Terrier I met on a nighttime walk in our condo neighborhood. Besides her sweet-natured disposition, I also admired her alert, upright ears and beautiful, intelligent eyes. Her owners told me they'd found her several months ago when the father and daughter of the family were jogging more than a mile from their home.

"When we first saw her we thought she was a dangerous wild dog. With her wet, terribly matted dirty coat and no collar it was obvious she'd been on her own for quite a while. I began talking to her to try to calm her down so we could pass by without her biting us. She settled down and, to our surprise, when we continued on our run, she jogged along with us the entire way home!"

"How did you decide to keep her?" I asked.

"I was immediately in love with this precious dog," the mom of the family told me. "I felt if she'd run all the way home with my husband and daughter then she wanted to belong to us. My husband wasn't keen on the idea of us having a dog, especially not this one."

"Well, tell her about Mia's dash through the neighborhood that first day she followed us home!" the husband challenged.

"It was really quite funny, as we looked back on the event later. Mia escaped out our back door and dashed into a nearby neighbor's house when guests were arriving for a party. The guests at the party thought she was the host's dog and the host thought she'd come with one of the guests! Everyone could see she was a mild-mannered dog even though she was a very dirty one! When we reached her and explained that she was a stray, several folks said they'd like to keep her if we weren't going to."

The husband continued the story. "I felt we needed to try to find her owners so I drove her to the dog shelter. They found an ID chip in her shoulder. That's how we knew her name was Mia. Her owners were notified but they never replied to the phone call or letter stating she'd been found. The Humane Society said folks often don't respond to found dog notices because they don't want to pay the fine or the boarding fee for having a loose dog."

"I put our name on the list to be called if the owners didn't come for her," the wife said. "When the required wait period had passed there was quite a long list of folks who wanted a Westie. I was elated to receive the call that we were first on the list and could come pick her up," the mom said.

The husband grudgingly agreed that Mia was well-behaved "most of the time" and easily settled into their life. "She turned out to be a jogger just like me and loves our early-morning runs together!" the husband declared as he rubbed the ears of the adoring dog.

What a lucky day it was for Mia when that kindhearted family found her! Oh, that every lost dog could be so fortunate!

Coco and Chanel were two Maltese beauties I met while walking in our neighborhood.

"Who are these two little darlings?" I asked the lady holding their leashes.

"Coco is my dog and Chanel belongs to a friend of mine. I often get to dog-sit her."

"Those elegant names certainly fit these two," I told her. "They're so similar in size and appearance. Are they from the same litter?" I asked.

"Yes, my friend bought Chanel as a puppy from a Maltese breeder in Pennsylvania and when her son and daughter-in-law met Chanel they wanted one just like her. They went to the breeder and bought her sister. My friend had never had a dog before but always wanted one she could name Chanel. She said that every Chanel needs a Coco so her son named his Maltese Coco."

The two "sisters" sat quietly watching us as if they were listening to our conversation. "They're certainly well-behaved dogs," I commented.

"We've been so happy to have Coco come live with us since her family had to give her up. We always said we loved Chanel like she was our own so they flew her sister down from Pennsylvania to Naples and we picked her up at the airport. It was love at first sight! She loves when Chanel comes to visit and play. We take Coco with us pretty much everywhere we go. Everyone who meets her loves her!"

Nicky was a darling little furry boy dog, reigning over a beautiful Naples gift shop. Tom and I were leaving the breakfast diner next door when I saw Nicky lying in the doorway of his shop. He was obviously a Pekingese with his over-the-back tail curl but had a close-cut grooming which made him look like a black and white bear cub.

I couldn't resist going into the shop to meet the formal, little guy. His owner explained that Nicky was a special breed called a tuxedo Pekingese. His legs, chest, and belly markings made him look like he was wearing a black tuxedo. Nicky reflected the elegance of the shop with his black-tie attire.

He stayed very close to his owner at all times and would not let anyone pet him until his owner said to him, "It's ok." Nicky is trained to do that to protect him from dognappers because many of these dogs are stolen from their owners.

Since that first meeting, I've "shopped" in that store often, just to visit the special little Nicky.

LePetite Cherie and *Mr. Tote* were miniature black poodles I met while riding my bike past their house. They were on the driveway, preparing for a car trip with their owner.

"What darling little dogs!" I exclaimed. As I petted and held each of them, their elegant mistress told me they lived a life of luxury and ease with all of their needs met … plus some. Both had regular spa appointments, and LePetite Cherie always came away with her nails painted! Their owner took regular airline and car trips, and both dogs traveled with her. They each had their own designer bags and would jump into their totes, ready to go, when they sensed an upcoming trip.

NOTE: I found the description of the little poodles' lifestyle to be very interesting and am happy for dogs who live in such luxury. I've learned that there are as many different types of dog lovers as there are breeds of dogs. Some owners lavish much attention on their own grooming with expensive hair, nail, and spa treatments as part of what they value. Those same people may be inclined to provide their dogs with the same lifestyle. Other owners and their dogs live a much more practical existence; the dogs are well cared for but don't receive constant first-class treatment. I believe all dogs give the same loyalty and devotion to their owners, regardless of what type of *loving* care is provided. Isn't their ability to adapt and accept one of the reasons we so love dogs?

Lulu was a small, black Pekingese who loved to chase rabbits in our neighborhood. Tom and I met her while out walking one night on our street. Her owner told me, "She is constantly on the alert during her bedtime nightly walk. She's hoping to spot a bunny that she can threaten with her barks."

Lulu was a sweet-natured, silky-coated little girl dog who showed her love to everyone by rolling onto her back for a tummy scratch, which she demonstrated for me on this, our first meeting. Wiggle, wiggle, paws in the air!

Lucy, a small, red-haired Pekingese, lived down the street from Lulu. They were great friends and spent time at each other's condos. They were both happiest when they were together, romping and playing. Lucy was shyer of strangers, although she tried to emulate Lulu's adventurous nature. After a few minutes of petting and crooning to her, Lucy gave in and freely welcomed my affectionate petting

Buster Brown was a brown and tan, long-haired shepherd/ Lab mix. His owners took him to their shoe store each day where he watched from the back room door as customers browsed among the shoes. The owners told me that he came to them as a "pound puppy" and, ten years later, was still the light of their lives.

"He is such a good dog and won't come into the store area unless he's invited or if he senses one of us is alone. He seems to know when he may need to guard us and the store. Then he keeps a sharp eye on all customers. Otherwise he appears to sleep away the day, seemingly unconcerned with anyone's comings and goings. When the UPS man comes in the front door, Buster always seems to know it and stands at attention, waiting for the treat which is always delivered to him with our UPS orders."

Annie was an unusually marked, black, gray, and brown spotted, long-haired dog who lived at an antique store. Her owners first saw her at the Humane Society and believed that her shepherd-like size made her too large for them. They felt that because they were at work every day, they wouldn't be able to have a dog.

After visiting her several times and at the encouragement of the Humane Society staff, they realized they could take the dog to their store each day. As the owners of the shop, who was going to tell them no? They found that Annie was a very polite, quiet, sweet dog in the shop. She mostly ignored customers until someone showed her some attention, and then she became most attentive to their petting. As I talked to Annie and petted her, she leaned into my legs and accepted my massages delightedly. What a darling, loyal girl!

Brooklyn was a small Boston terrier I met at a sidewalk bistro. He'd been sitting inconspicuously on his mistress's lap throughout most of the meal. When dessert was delivered to the table, Brooklyn lifted his head and sniffed politely.

"He loves the smell of chocolate," she reported to me. "I paid three hundred dollars for him over the Internet. We drove four hours from our home to pick him up. He's been worth every penny … such a nice boy.

"You should consider owning a Boston terrier. Brooklyn is the third one I've had, and I really think they're the best dog. No problem at all to care for. He loves everyone, eventually, after being very protective of me. He sometimes growls at strangers but rarely barks."

Bentley, a miniature white poodle, was "gifted" to a neighbor on our street in Naples. She didn't want the responsibility of dog ownership. However, her family and friends, all dog lovers, believed she needed a dog for companionship. So Bentley was given to her on a "trial basis."

At the tender age of three months, Bentley, a rambunctious and difficult little dog, had already been shuttled between two homes. He needed almost constant attention and was traumatized when left alone, even briefly. However, with loving attention and after many weeks of training for both dog and owner, Bentley became the darling of the entire neighborhood.

"I don't think anyone should ever give a dog as a gift, but I would not like to be without him now. I love him so much!" his owner told me when I first met Bentley on our driveway and learned the story of his origin.

Talleen was a small blond and brown pug I met while I was walking in our neighborhood. She strutted along with her tail curled over her back, expecting and receiving greetings from everyone walking by. She was such a little wiggly bundle of sweetness that it was difficult not to stop to give her a pet and massage. Her owner explained that the name Talleen means "pretty girl." How appropriate! If anyone tried to walk past her without a pet and chat, Talleen barked at them until they showed her some attention or were out of sight!

Lily was a small white and tan sheltie mix with pointed ears. Her owner was surprised when Lily barked at me as I approached on the sidewalk near a Naples dress shop.

"Maybe she thought you were going to walk by without greeting her," the owner said.

I stopped to let Lily sniff my hand in greeting. "She has a beautiful coat and such a sweet disposition!" I said. Lily proceeded to turn from side to side for an all-over scratch and massage.

Her elderly lady owner said to me, "I'm worried about Lily. All night long she wouldn't lay her head down but kept it up and turned to the side. I think she's got a pinched nerve in her neck. I'm taking her to the vet today to see what the problem is."

As is often the case in these brief dog encounters, comments come from seemingly out of the blue. I usually offer a statement of interest or concern, such as in this case, "Well, the poor little thing. Good luck with Lily's vet visit!" as I continue on past.

Molly was an all-white Lhasa Apso I met while walking toward a food market.

"Well, what's this little champion's name?" I asked the lady sitting on a bench with her outside the market.

The lady told me that Molly loves people and is especially happy when the owner's adult children come to visit. "Molly can sleep all day, every day, but when the family or other guests arrive, she is a bundle of energy," she said. "Just like me, I think!"

Many active, retired people live in Naples with dogs who, I believe, help them remain energized.

Moose was a shaggy-coated Labradoodle Tom and I met while riding our bicycles in a beautiful lake community in Naples. "What an unusually wonderful looking dog!" was my introductory comment.

"He gets a lot of attention. Our other dog was a Lab and just great. This one is a Labradoodle, part Lab and part poodle. He doesn't shed. It's like not having a dog at all—no dog hairs all over the place," the owner explained.

While I cuddled the loving little guy, I asked his age.

"He's only sixteen months old—still a pup, actually—but very well-behaved," his owner replied.

"His coat is so soft, and I've never seen a dog this color before," I said.

"He's an apricot color and very rare for a Lab-poodle mix," the owner said.

"Well, he's certainly a sweetheart of a dog," I said as Moose wiggled for more pets.

"He's an observer," the owner said. "He likes to watch kids on bikes, ducks on the lakes, and people walking by, but he rarely barks. He just sits alertly and observes."

During our brief meeting with Moose, he quietly demonstrated that he's definitely an observer.

Bosox, a Boston terrier, was on a leash outside a pizza shop with his owners. While petting his sleek, black coat, I was told that he was only a puppy, just six weeks old.

"We live in a condo, and even though we've had big dogs before, Bosox is just the right size for us and our place. We've seen big dogs living in condo communities where there is no place for them to exercise, and they spend their lives living in small spaces. I think it's cruel. Bosox can run around in our condo and get some exercise, but we'll walk him every day too."

The parents and ten-year-old son obviously doted on the dog, so I asked them who Bosox sleeps with. The parents looked at their son, who quickly said, "We just picked him up from the breeder this afternoon, and he'll sleep with me!" Ah, one lucky little boy and a happy dog.

Ginger was a medium-sized, blond-haired bundle of cuddly dog. When I met her while out walking, she bounded to the end of her leash to sniff and lick my hand. Then she ran back to her owner, sat down, and barked at me ferociously!

I continued to talk and coo to her. She ran back to me with a wiggle and wag, licking my hand and circling my feet joyfully. Then, back to her owner to again bark aggressively at me.

"She so wants to be a big, mean guard dog, but her true nature always wins out, and she greets everyone she meets with that enthusiastic welcome," her owner said.

Izzy had a short-haired coat befitting her shepherd-pug lineage. While she sat in a shopping cart at a large crafts store, I petted her and admired her "sidelights," the blond patches on her shoulders.

"Because of the light-colored stripe down her back, we call her our little skunk. She is so fun, always making us laugh!" her owner told me.

"Izzy is such a sweet dog. Do you often take her with you into stores?" I asked.

The mom and two school-aged daughters made the following quick comments: "She goes just about everywhere with us." "Izzy's so small and no trouble." "I think most shop owners don't even notice her because she almost never barks."

The mom then added, "I've never been asked to take her outside. Of course I'd never take her into Publix (a large Naples-area food market chain)."

Jezebel crawled onto the lap of her owner and hung half out of the open van window to visit with me as I was walking by a McDonald's drive-through.

"She's only six months old and is so good. She's a Jack Russell–fox terrier mix, but we think there's some dachshund in her too. Look how long she is in the body. I found her at the shelter and immediately fell in love with her pale gray eyes. Isn't she beautiful?"

I readily agreed as the sweet little black and white dog kissed me all over my face while I petted her. What a lucky owner and a delightful dog!

Oreo was a husky-malamute dog I met on yet another early morning walk. His owner was surprised that he so quickly leaned into me for massages and pets. She said usually he's very aloof with strangers.

"You must be a dog person, and Oreo senses it," she told me.

As I massaged his shoulders and hips, she apologized for his massive shedding.

"I don't mind a bit," I told her. I'd not yet had my dog fix on that morning's walk, and I welcomed Oreo's obvious joy at my attention to him.

Toby was a small, white, poodle–shih tzu mix. His owner was giving him an early morning walk, and Toby was trotting ahead, definitely in charge.

"He's my first dog ever," his owner told me.

As I stooped to pet him, it was obvious Toby wanted me to pick him up.

"Yes, you can hold him. He loves to give kisses! In fact his groomers tell me Toby is the 'kissingest' dog they've ever seen!"

What a joy to cuddle the little guy while he kissed my face all over.

Barney was a miniature beagle. As I approached him on the sidewalk outside a Naples library, he cautiously sniffed me and shyly circled my legs before sitting up for me to pick him up.

I was so overcome with praise and cooing to him that his owner, with much exasperation in her voice, asked, "Do you want him?" She then explained that even after ten months, he still raced over furniture and tore around her condo several times a day. With his small, adorable beagle shape and coloring, he seemed to me to be a perfect dog.

His owner was only joking about giving him away because she then praised him for being such a good walker on the leash.

"We're hoping continuing obedience classes and more frequent exercising will help Barney become less 'hurricane-ish' in our condo. Naples has enough of those!" Barney's owner said with a laugh.

Rocky and *Bucky* were two small tan dogs who looked quite different from each other, but I learned they were brothers from the same litter. Rocky was wire haired, and Bucky was short haired and smooth coated. Tom and I met them while walking on the boardwalk approach to Vanderbilt Beach.

While they were leaping and growling at each other, both trying to get the most pets and massages from me, I learned the following from their owner, who was trying to keep their leashes untangled from around his ankles: "Rocky and Bucky have been our two boys for the last couple of years. Today I'm walking them so Mommy can stay in bed for a while longer. We're expecting our first baby in two weeks. As you can see, these two are so jealous of each other and argue and growl about who is getting the most attention from us. They're in for a surprise when the baby arrives!"

At the "sit" command, they both sat contentedly and let me pet them.

"I hope they adjust well and become good 'big brothers' to the new baby," I said before we continued on our walk.

Cleopatra and ***Latifah*** were two dogs I "met" while shopping for postcards.

I overheard a lady nearby say to her friend, "This card looks just like our Cleo!"

I asked her about Cleo, and she joyfully related the following: "Cleopatra and Latifah are our two black and white poodles who are prize-winning queens." Motioning to the other lady with her, she continued, "We enter them in dog shows, and they often win or place."

Just like a proud parent, she reached into her purse and pulled forth a small album and began showing me photos of her two queens.

"We're both retired now, and Cleopatra and Latifah are the center of our life. We enjoy entering them in dog shows across the country. They've each won several dog food commercial contests. Aren't they beauties?"

I assured her they were both quite royal! Through their photos and owners' descriptions of them, I felt I had actually met these two poodles, so into my "Dogs I've Met" journal they went!

SPAIN

While leading a group of ten women friends on a tour of Spain I saw many well-tended boxers, bassets, collies and other breeds of dogs being walked by their owners. Although I wasn't able to meet any of these dogs, I was fortunate to become acquainted with one special black puppy of questionable-heritage. It all started when Virgil, the driver of our private bus, found three round-bellied, maybe two-month-old puppies abandoned in a parking lot near our hotel in Seville. He and two other soft-hearted drivers each rescued one of the puppies.

Virgil came to me and asked, "Jessie, I've found a little stray pup that I'd like to take home to my sons in Madrid. Would it be alright with you if he rides on the bus with us these last three days of the tour? I really couldn't leave him abandoned at the bus lot and he's a well-behaved little pup."

My friends laughed because they knew what my answer would be to any question regarding a dog. When I determined that nobody in my group objected to another "passenger" or was allergic to dogs, of course I said, "Yes, but only if the puppy rides with me!"

Jesse became the most popular canine in Spain! Each of us cuddled and cared for him as we continued our tour. Virgil named him Jesse, the masculine form of my name, in appreciation for my willingness to bring him along. Since this would be the fourth time I'd had a dog named for me, we decided his formal name should be Jesse IV.

When he first joined us, Jesse was quite a dusty little guy but I didn't mind his paw prints on my clothes when I held him on my lap. However, Virgil purchased a new bed sheet for me to cover myself with until Jesse could have his first bath at a bus washing station.

Jesse was easy to "bus train," because we made frequent stops and would always give him a "watering" on his new leash. We happily referred to him our "small dog" and only once on the bus did we have to call him our "wee" dog. He entertained us as he scampered up and down the aisle of the bus. All of his rolling, jumping and tumbling puppy antics tired him out each day. He'd nap on my lap while we were riding along, but at night he would go quietly into the cozy bed Virgil created for him in a storage area of the bus.

Jesse was a most welcome addition to our traveling group and made the final days of our tour through Ronda, Marbella and Granada especially fun. My memories of beautiful southern Spain will always be intertwined with thoughts of little Jesse IV's puppy kisses and the pleasure of traveling along with him wiggling in my arms or snoozing on my lap.

Dogs I Know

Wally
Columbus, Ohio

"My goal in life is to be as good of a person as
my dog already thinks I am."   *Unknown*

Albert
Gahanna, Ohio

"He hath a share of man's intelligence but no share of man's falsehood."   *Sir Walter Scott*

Zoe
Naples, Florida

"A good dog deserves a good home."   *Proverb*

Chloe
Hilliard, Ohio

"To err is human, to forgive, canine." Unknown

SALEM, OHIO

Tom and I often visit family in Salem, a beautiful small town with many trees and a large park, in northeastern Ohio. There are numerous dogs out and about when I walk there. The following are some of the Salem, Ohio dogs I've met and noted in my journal:

Lucy was a beautiful yellow Lab who welcomed pats and crooning from strangers. She was walking with her owner but swiveled her head toward me as I approached on the sidewalk. With a wiggling wag, she let me know that a visit and massage was in order.

Her owner told me that Lucy is an excellent dog, although her previous owners were inaccurate when they said she hardly sheds. Lucy's coat was sleek, and she shed very little simply because her owner had the time to brush her, and enjoyed doing so, several times a day.

I was sorry to learn they may have to find another home for Lucy because her present owners weren't going to be able to walk her daily once winter came. They hoped their daughter, who owned Lucy's sister, would take Lucy also. That was good news for Lucy, who would remain with her family.

Bentley was another beautiful pale yellow Lab who I first thought was Lucy when I saw him walking in the same neighborhood. (Maybe, because he was male, I should say he was handsome instead of beautiful.) His owner told me, "He goes camping with us—even joined us on a fly-in wilderness camp in Alaska. He loves the outdoors."

Ellie was a black Lab. Her friendly disposition was constant except when the mailman would appear on the street. With a threatening bark and growl from inside the house or outside at her tie-down, she tried her best to get to him. Ellie was the sweetest, most affectionate dog with everyone else. Did a mailman traumatize her sometime that her owners didn't know about? Ellie was adopted from a dog shelter, so the family doesn't know the source of that behavior with the mailman.

Ellie's other condition couldn't seem to be cured, even after many vet visits. At the mature age of four, she continued her puppy habit of uncontrolled wetting in joy around the feet of unsuspecting guests. When I first met Ellie on their driveway, I was warned to step back while she did her wiggling, wet welcome. Ellie rolled onto her side and then onto her back to let me rub her belly.

As so often happens with our sweet dogs, everyone who knew and cherished Ellie simply overlooked her occasional "bad dog" side while accepting and loving her "good dog" personality.

Sammy was a small Boston terrier who was in his front lawn as I was walking past. "What a handsome, little tough guy," I called out to his owner.

I was told that Sammy was purchased from a pet store where he lived for several months. His siblings had been sold quickly, but Sammy had a hernia, and after surgery nobody was interested in buying him.

The young married couple who owned him took turns giving the following information about Sammy: "He was so cute, but we weren't permitted to have a dog in our apartment. We visited him regularly at the pet store, and on the day we had the closing for our house, we celebrated by buying Sammy and bringing him home too!

"He is such a good dog. He barks at anyone who comes into our yard but quickly settles down, except if the person is wearing sunglasses. We've not figured out why he doesn't like people wearing sunglasses! He is such a good dog.

"I love his blond color. I think he must have some black terrier in him too because his face and ears are black. Don't you just love his soft ears?"

While I held and cuddled him, his master continued. "Our only problem has been his fleas that we can't seem to get rid of. We've tried several treatments." I sat him down quickly and, with a gentle pat on his head, encouraged them to keep trying. (I tried to not "flee" away too rudely!)

Opal was a large, long-haired blond Samoyed-Akita mix whom I met at a garage sale in Salem.

Her owner told me the following story of Opal's origin: "I got Opal at another garage sale in my neighborhood last year. The lady having the sale handed me her dog's leash and told me she sees me walking every day and she thinks I need the dog. I told her she could hire someone to walk her dog. She explained that she didn't want me to just *walk* the dog, but that she wanted me to *keep* the dog. She was moving into an apartment and had to find a new home for Opal.

"It's been a great arrangement because Opal is a really good dog. But she's still a puppy with a puppy's almost constantly playful attitude."

I was happy to hold Opal on her leash and pet her while her owner shopped at the garage sale.

KENYA

A three-week tour of Kenya with a group of five Swahili language students from my school was all I'd hoped for and more. The students and I were enthralled with the beauty of the people, the variety of geography and the fascinating sights from Nairobi to the Masai Mara and from Mombasa to Lamu. Since this was my second visit to Kenya, I was fortunate to have friends there who coordinated home stays for our first week. Something I didn't expect my home stay to include was getting to meet two interesting dogs.

Kenyan friends had told me that the place of dogs in the culture is different from that in the United States. Dogs are usually not looked upon as pets and often aren't even given names. They are kept for protection and are rarely cuddled or brought into the house. Similar to what I've found in many places in the world, the value of dogs is determined by the service they can give people. The warm welcome I received from my host family became even more delightful for me when I discovered they had two dogs *with names!*

Snoopy and **Brandy** were guard dogs who usually roamed freely inside the fence of the family's compound. They were only tied at their doghouses when visitors were expected. Those two hard-working dogs growled and barked if strangers tried to come into the yard. They also kept the compound secure from snakes, small rodents and gazelles that frequented the farm area.

"What are their names?" was my first question when I saw the dogs. The family was puzzled by my interest until I explained that I had a dog at home. I told them about Cameron, our only dog at that time. "He's only a pet but he does like to chase and sometimes capture small varmints at our farm in Ohio."

When I travel with students, I always require that they carry a small album of photos which represent their home life in the United States. I model this practice by carrying my own photo album. In my album, I had a photo of Cameron that I shared with the Kenyan family to help them understand his important place in my life.

I was amused to learn that Snoopy, the brown and white German shepherd, was named for Charlie Brown's dog. Brandy was a red-coated, long-legged dog who, along with Snoopy, received an occasional pet and cuddle from the young daughters in the family. The parents, however, did not show affection for the dogs but called praises to them when they performed good security duties and scolded them when they barked unnecessarily.

There were few opportunities for me to interact with Snoopy and Brandy as we came and went from the farm into Nairobi and on excursions with my students. However, meeting these two hard-working dogs is a sweet memory, among my unparalleled recollections of Kenya.

HILLIARD, OHIO

During the summer months, Tom and I live on our small farm near Hilliard, a suburb of Columbus in central Ohio. It was here that we enjoyed the company of our three dogs, Cameron, Trixster, and Simba, for several years. Since the loss of each of them over a three-year period, I began noting in my journal the names and information about other dogs I meet in the area. These are some of them:

Tucker was a small, blond, wire-haired little sweetie who loved barking behind his invisible fence. He barked at anyone who passed on the street in front of or behind his house, doing his best as a little dog to do the big job of guarding his domain.

His owner, a young girl, talked to me about Tucker as I was walking by their house. "He's a goofy dog, but we all like him a lot." I didn't learn what makes him "goofy."

White Paws was a medium-sized Shiba Inu. His brushy tail, small, pointed ears, and red coat gave him the look of a little fox. He was such a handsome dog that I couldn't possibly walk past him without a comment, even though I could see his owners were trying hard to help him walk better on his leash. "He looks like a strong little fox," I told them.

The couple and their little daughter stopped. While White Paws sat, I learned the following: "After many obedience lessons, White Paws has become quite the little gentleman, sitting quietly while we chat with neighbors we meet on nightly walks. Before obedience classes he would leap, pull, lunge, and circle around our legs when we attempted to walk him. Now he knows all the important commands: sit, stay, and heel.

"Obedience classes are worth every penny if you want a nice, mannerly dog," White Paws's owners exclaimed.

"How did he get the name White Paws?" I asked.

"You can see he has two white paws, and we let our daughter name him."

Cheyenne was a mostly black shepherd who lived on the road where Tom and I walk almost daily. She quietly lay outside the garage door, guarding the driveway of her home, only standing to bark if walkers come too near her lawn.

Her owners talked to us, sharing the following traits of their Cheyenne: Her favorite play activity was to dive into the pond near her house to retrieve small rocks that were thrown there. "Chey" would disappear under water for several seconds, digging until she found the exact rock that was thrown, retrieve it, and drop it at the feet of her owner, waiting to dive again.

Her only threatening behavior came when the neighborhood cats walked too near her driveway. She would lie down on her tummy, back paws poised, ready to charge if they came too close. The couple of times the cats dared to venture inside her invisible fence, Chey merely played with them, presenting no threat at all. Such a fun, good dog.

Biff was a six-year-old 10-pound Pomeranian. His salt and pepper coat closely matched his mistress's hair, making the two of them a quite striking pair.

When I admired him as I walked by her parked car at a plant nursery, Biff's owner proudly lifted him out of her car to introduce him to me. She then related the following: "He was a stray that I found. I should have known not to bring such a darling dog into my house. I had intended to find an owner for him because I'm not a dog person. However, who could resist such a sweet little fellow as him?

"Some folks say he looks like a bear. Others have said a raccoon, and some say he looks just like an otter. Most Pomeranians have a fluffy tail that curves over their backs. Biff's tail is more of an exploding Brillo pad!

"I named him Biff because he's such a big macho man! There could be no better dog to have than this one. He eats very little so is a most inexpensive dog to feed. And his poops are so small I have to watch where he goes and pick them up immediately or I'd lose them in the grass. He is such a gentleman. Everyone just loves him!"

NOTE: Biff's is definitely one of the most memorable and interesting dog bios I've collected. In fact, this delightful encounter gave me the idea to be more purposeful in writing about the dogs I meet, not just when traveling, but also when nearer home.

Snoopy and *Buddy* were walking in a park with their owner. When I asked if I could talk to the dogs, the owner said, "Buddy (a black Lab) is very friendly, but Snoopy (a gray and white beagle-basset mix) doesn't always like strangers."

I began talking to the pair, telling them how handsome I thought they were. Buddy immediately sniffed me and welcomed a pat and cuddle. Snoopy gave an almost imperceptible deep growl, letting me know he didn't trust me. I again stated how handsome they were and walked on. Good dogs!

Bourbon was a 40-pound Humane Society adoptee. His lineage included Akita, German shepherd, and chow. I was happy to meet Bourbon when he came with his owner on a visit to our farm.

While Bourbon romped and ran, enjoying the wide open spaces of our lawn and fields, his owner related the following to me: "I visited the Humane Society several times, looking for a dog. I wanted a medium-sized dog and was first told that Bourbon was considered a large dog. After determining that he was already full grown at 40 pounds, I decided I would adopt him.

"He'd been looking at me lovingly, running to the front of the cage every time I visited. I knew he was the dog for me.

"He had been *given* the name 'Rocky,' but I wanted a classier name. A friend suggested 'Whiskey' because of his brown-shaded coat. He is so well behaved I knew he would need a more posh name, so I chose 'Bourbon.' He recognized the name immediately and always comes when I call him."

She demonstrated that several times by calling his name. Like a good, well-trained, much-loved dog, he came directly to her every time. Of course, he always got much praise and many loving pats. Good boy!

Miss Bailey was a blond-coated shepherd/Lab mix who visited Tom and me at our farm with her master. We learned the following about Miss Bailey: "She is best friends with Caesar, a German Shepherd and Rottweiler mix, who also comes to my office every day with his owner. We're both fortunate to be able to bring our dogs with us to the Campus Ministry Center where we work. They do enjoy each other, and we know they're healthier dogs because of the exercise their play gives them.

"**Caesar** is older and much bigger than Bailey, but she is definitely the alpha dog in their friendship. She loves to grab at his legs or short stubby tail and then run away under a table where he can't fit. Caesar takes Bailey's abuse for just so long and then growls at her. She seems to understand she needs to back off a bit, so she lies down beside him and relaxes. She is an ornery, fun-loving little girl and really smart!"

Goliath was one of the largest dogs I've ever met. When Tom and I first saw him from a distance, we weren't sure that he *was* a dog. He was about the height of a Shetland pony and almost as broad. This sweet-natured Saint Bernard greeted us with a total body wag as we approached him on our evening walk in a city park.

"Goliath doesn't know how large he is, so be careful that he doesn't upset you," his owner warned as she held him on his leash. Goliath leaned into me with great affection as I massaged and cooed to him. Such a nice, *big* dog!

Daisy was a chubby English bulldog whom I saw waddling along a busy, two-lane highway. I pulled into the nearest driveway, got out of my car, squatted down, and called to the dog. She barreled to me, dropped down, and rolled over, very happy for me to rub her belly.

The homes were situated off the road in a wooded area, and I didn't feel comfortable walking close enough to knock on a door. I gave my loudest whistle, hoping someone from one of the nearby houses would come outside and rescue the little dog. Finally I walked nearer to one of the houses and whistled really loudly outside the open garage door.

A teenage boy came out and said, "Oh, that's Daisy. She lives two houses away and often escapes from their yard."

With cars whizzing by at the end of the driveways, I wanted to be sure Daisy was safe. She obviously knew the boy and waddled along beside him as he walked her to her yard. I returned to my car, happy that I didn't have to search further for Daisy's owners. I hope her owners will do a better job of keeping her away from that busy roadway.

Cuervo was a rescued dog from the Humane Society. I met her outside a Meijer department store where she was lying in the grass waiting patiently for her mistress to return. Her master was sitting nearby, waiting also. Cuervo tolerated me talking to her and massaging her shoulders, but she kept her eyes alertly trained on the door of the store.

While I petted and crooned to her, I got teary-eyed because she looked so much like my big yellow Simba, whom I'd been without for about six months. With the same light blond shoulder markings and brown "eyeliner" eyes, it was almost like petting Simba.

As I talked about her to her owner, I learned that she has many of Simba's traits.

"She is very protective of my wife," Cuervo's master said. "We keep a muzzle on her when we go camping because she will nip at folks who walk too close, and she especially likes to growl and even lunge at dogs that walk near."

When I asked how she was given the name Cuervo, I was told the following: "My daughter's college was having an alcohol search of the dorms. In order to keep it from being confiscated, she brought home a huge jug of Cuervo. We'd been trying to think of a name for our then-new dog, and we saw that jug sitting on the kitchen counter and decided that would be a good name for her."

I know people have interesting reasons for pet name choices, but naming such a beautiful, loyal dog after a type of alcohol left a bad taste in my mouth. Of course, I've never tasted Cuervo, so what do I know?

Ditka was a black Lab whom I met while visiting a hospitalized friend. He was in the lobby with his owner, a hospital volunteer. She told me that he was named for, of course, the

Chicago Bears' Mike Ditka. However, a more interesting thing about Ditka, the Labrador, was that he had been a therapy dog for six years.

On the day I met him, he was dressed as a construction worker complete with a lightweight tool belt over his back and a small yellow hardhat on his head. This attire was in recognition of the monumental construction project going on around the entrance to the hospital.

I could see that Ditka made people smile wherever he went. Construction workers passing inside the lobby showed their appreciation of his solidarity. One called out, "Does he have a union card?"

His owner laughed when she said that she thinks it's "so ridiculous" the way everyone notices Ditka. I felt she liked the attention she received as Ditka's very creative owner. She enjoyed dressing him in outfits to suit different occasions.

Ditka "worked" the children's area of the hospital and was on call when a patient's family requested that he pay a visit. His job was to be himself, quietly letting his presence be felt by laying his head on the side of the bed, accepting whatever attention was given. Especially with children and the elderly, Ditka's emotional support was immeasurable.

I felt lucky to have chanced upon Ditka and his owner, both giving such invaluable volunteer service.

Sophie was a 1½-year-old beagle who was lying alone in the shade at a church festival Tom and I attended. She had no leash, and there seemed to be no owner in sight, so I sat down on the ground next to her, petting and talking to her. She crawled onto my lap, quite comfortable with my attention. After much too short of a time, her owner returned.

He'd been working at an iced tea stand nearby, keeping an eye on her (and me, I'm sure).

He told me that Sophie had been quiet and ladylike since she was a puppy. Unlike many beagles, she rarely barked or "followed her nose" wherever it led her. She stayed close to him or whoever was tending her. I enjoyed my visit with her so much that I was hoping I'd be the one tending her longer than just the fifteen minutes I was given.

Tom and I have often said beagles are our favorite breed, and little Sophie was the most perfect one we'd ever seen.

Although she didn't look much like our "beagle-ish" Cameron, who we'd been without for a couple of years at that time, I did think of him while petting her. Cameron would never have sat still outside anywhere without a leash. He would have loved the petting and affectionate cuddle, but his very favorite activity outside was to always be "following his nose" to something somewhere else. Ah, how I miss that dear boy dog!

Sandy was a beautiful golden retriever–shepherd mix who was being walked by her owner at the same church festival where I met Sophie. All I had to do was pause and smile at her, and she leaned into my legs for a pet.

"What a precious one!" I told the mother with the young daughter who was holding her leash. I learned that the breeder had told the family that Sandy would grow to be no more than 40 to 60 pounds. They were hoping for 40 pounds, but when I met her, she weighed a bit over 100 pounds!

"What a surprise to learn that the old adage about large-footed puppies growing into big dogs is true!" the mother said. "I guess we were overly trusting of the breeder's promise about Sandy's grown-up size."

Montana and *Freedom* were well-traveled dogs who stopped in at our farm for a too-short afternoon visit with their owners, Tom's cousins. Riding in their special area of the fifth-wheel pickup truck with a camper trailer, Montana and Freedom had made several cross-country camping trips with their owners.

These two large shepherd-mix dogs exemplify the belief that every dog needs a buddy. "It's difficult to determine the alpha dog in this pair. They seem to exchange that role between them as they romp, roll, run, and lavish affection on each other and us," their owners explained.

What fun it was to see those two big dogs chasing around our pond and fields.

WALNUT CREEK, OHIO

When visiting my sister in the small village of Walnut Creek in the Amish area of Holmes County, Ohio, I've been fortunate to meet these dogs:

Rosie was a yellow Lab who lived part time at an assisted living center. She was a hard-working, silky-coated beauty who lovingly greeted all residents and guests with a quiet gentleness. She calmly trotted from room to room, laying her head in a lap or on the edge of a bed. Rosie seemed to instinctively know who needed her attention. The residents welcomed her loving attention. Most of them patted her head or spoke to her warmly.

Signs posted throughout the facility asking residents and visitors to "PLEASE DON'T FEED ROSIE." It seemed too many folks liked to reward her good works with treats, and Rosie had been gaining weight.

Her owner worked at the center and often instructed Rosie to go into her crate in the crafts room during lunch and afternoon snack time. Rosie did that quite willingly and used the time to nap. Each day she came to work and then went with her owner to their home nearby. Like all the other staff at the center, Rosie took her job seriously, spreading cheer and comfort to everyone she met.

Jack was, of course, a Jack Russell terrier. I met him at a large farmers market in Walnut Creek.

His owner shared that he was the "smartest dog ever." Jack knew when it was time to walk, so he would gather the walking shoes and his leash and lay them at his owner's feet.

When I asked where Jack sleeps, his owner answered, "With us on our bed, of course. We love him so much!"

I smiled, remembering how my own Cameron, and sometimes Simba, loved to sleep with us on our bed. When Trixster came to live with Tom and me, we would sometimes have a "three-dog night."

Duke was a four-year-old black standard poodle. His owner told me that they had had him in obedience classes for four years.

I'm not sure why Duke needed four years of classes because he appeared to be totally obedient. He was lying at his owner's feet, alertly watching while a throng of people walked around him, shopping and talking. I commented to his owner that even though she wasn't holding his leash, Duke continued to lie quietly in his tensely alert position.

"He is in the 'stay' position and will not break from that until I give him the signal," she explained.

Just then, Duke stood and strolled away! A man walking toward him attracted his attention, so Duke walked over to him and stood looking up.

Duke got a gentle scolding from his owner. "You were not to break without my signal!"

She brought him back to where I was standing, told him to "sit," and he laid down, very much in charge of himself (and his owner). *Another* year of obedience classes?

PERU

During a tour of Peru with a group of nine friends, I saw hundreds of mangy, dirty, dusty dogs. In every large city and small town there are many stray dogs. Even the few who had collars were seemingly alone, walking or running along with no owner evident. Being the dog-lover I am, it was distressing to see so many dogs lolling about or searching for food. Just like those I'd seen in Greece, these dogs were not approachable. However, I did get to spend about four hours with one dog in Peru.

Chico was a yellow, shaggy-coated, medium-sized hound who walked with our group as we made the three-hour hike to the Sun Gate overlooking Machu Picchu. We learned from one of the guides that Chico wasn't exactly a stray. Even though he had no collar and was on his own to find food and water during the day, he slept most nights in the shelter used by the Inca Trail guides.

Chico was a savvy trail dog. He'd run ahead to climb for a while with the hikers in the lead and then loop back to walk briefly with those in the rear of the group. Chico was acutely aware of who would be stopping to rest and have a snack. He'd be right there, with a pathetic whine and a paw held up, hoping for a bite.

Twice during the climb my friends and I had to stand to the side of the narrow trail to make space for a stretcher to be carried past with a hiker who'd been injured or overcome with altitude sickness. Each time, Chico sat like a statue, respectfully waiting and watching as the injured persons were carried past. We commented on the fact that many dogs would have barked and leaped at the porters who were running quickly down the trail. Chico seemed to understand the seriousness of the situation and maintained a quiet demeanor.

After arriving at the Sun Gate and taking many photos of the beautiful view, we relaxed and began snacking more seriously. Chico walked among us, welcoming any bite of apple, banana, cracker, or cookie offered to him. Then, when he realized our snacking was finished, he prepared for a nap. He worked for several minutes scratching up a pile of leaves in one corner of the Sun Gate wall and lay down to sleep. He slept soundly, snoring softly for about 20 minutes, and then began the climb back down the trail, probably looking for the next group he could "guide" to the top.

I'll always remember Chico as a smart, well-adjusted dog, making the best of his situation. After watching him working his way through that day, I can no longer think of him as a *stray* dog but rather as an *independent* dog.

ITALY

One of my pleasures in retirement is to plan and lead international tours for myself and small groups of friends.

During a twelve-day tour of Italy with eleven friends, I saw dogs every day. Most of them seemed to be strays with no collars or owners with them. There were only three times when the place and the situation permitted me to interact with owners and their dogs.

MANAROLA, ITALY

Kim was a tan, shaggy-coated, sweet-faced little mutt whom I met in this lovely village in the Cinque Terre region of northern Italy.

"What a sweet little baby. Does she speak English?" I asked the lady holding her on a leash.

"Her name's not Baby, it's Kim, and she only speaks Italian," her owner told me with a laugh.

I learned that the two-year-old dog had been a stray that the lady fed for several days outside her home and finally took inside to be her dog. My group was making a long walk to the next village, so that was the extent of information I found out about Kim during this brief meeting.

NOTE: As the curriculum coordinator at an international studies and foreign languages middle school during my last fourteen years before retirement, I've been interested in many languages. I've often wondered whether dogs could learn to respond to commands when spoken in different languages.

Tom and I have hosted many international guests in our home in Ohio. Japanese friends and their eight-year-old daughter once spent ten days with us. Their daughter, Mizuho, loved our three dogs but especially bonded with the smallest one, Trixster. He was about twelve years old at that time, and Mizuho was able to teach him to sit when she said, "Osuwari!" which is "sit" in Japanese.

A Kenyan friend was living with us for a year when I rescued Simba from my schoolyard. She often spoke to him in Kiswahili, and he seemed to understand and respond to her.

Is this teaching old dogs new tricks? Or are dogs smart enough to do what we want merely from the inflection in our voices? Who knows. I find it amusing and interesting to think about.

RIOMAGGIORE, ITALY

Tex, a blond Shepherd mix, was sitting with his owner, a twelve- or thirteen-year-old girl, watching tourists stroll through his beautiful Cinque Terre town. I paused to admire him and asked, "What is your dog's name?"

When she told me "Tex," I, of course, wanted to know how an Italian dog got the name Tex.

"I like reading about Texas in the United States," she happily told me. "I think he is a cowboy!" What a charming girl and delightful dog!

VENICE, ITALY

Tessie was an Italian greyhound, which is a miniature breed of greyhound. I met her on a chilly, windy night waiting for a vaporetto on the Grand Canal. While Tessie shivered under her owner's shawl, I was told, "Tessie is four years old. She is such a good dog, and we just can't leave her home. We would miss her so much.

"She always travels with us, and she especially loves coming to Italy, but she doesn't like this unseasonably cold night here now. This is Tessie's third trip to Italy."

I asked where they lived. "Kansas City" was the surprising reply. Who would guess I'd meet a Kansas dog in Venice? Of course, Tessie was an *Italian* greyhound!

*****

Angel was a medium-sized little girl dog whom I met on one of our trips home to Ohio from Florida. I was especially pleased to meet her because she looked so much like my Simba, and because it was during the first year of his death, I liked her name. I believe our dogs go to heaven, and if they become angels, my Simba is one!

The little dog was lapping water from a coffee cup held by her owner who told me Angel was four years old. "She was left outside my vet's office in a cardboard box with five littermates. My vet found homes for all of them, and I got Angel. She's the best dog. She is the perfect size for living in my small house and traveling with me—not too big and not too small—just perfect.

"I brush her often, so she sheds very little. I like to brush her."

While admiring Angel's yellow coat and dark-rimmed eyes, I thought of my loyal Simba and what a perfect "angel" he'd been for me also.

*****

REMEMBERING SIMBA

As I close out this journal of dog meetings, I'm remembering the many fine qualities of our last dog, Simba. I think of him most often because he was the dog we had the longest. For about two years he was our only dog, because Cameron and Trixster had died before him. Also, Simba was the only one we had to euthanize because of his cancer, and dog owners know the pain that experience causes, pain that is very difficult to get past.

Simba lived with Tom and me at our farm where he could roam freely, so I rarely had him on a leash or walked with him anywhere that we'd meet anyone whom I could talk to about him. However, I did talk about Simba often to our friends when they'd come to visit or when I'd miss him on my travels. As a healing practice, I'll recall some of what I often said about him:

Simba was given that name because Swahili is one of the languages taught at my school and "simba" means "lion." Since the popularity of *The Lion King*, most people probably know that fact. The name "Simba" seemed most appropriate because of his yellow coat and broad head and face.

I gave him the middle name of "Leon" because that was the middle name of the student who most encouraged me to take Simba home from the schoolyard where he'd been abandoned.

Even with his seemingly boundless devotion there was one trick Simba would try to pull on me. He loved to lie nearby while I worked in the flower beds. He would nap in the shade but quickly got up to follow me if I went to the shed or into the garage.

His trick was to occasionally try to leave my sight and walk the quarter mile down our lane to visit another dog who lived nearby. I'd look up from my work and not be able to find him. Then I'd begin searching and calling his name. Usually, he would come skulking from tree to tree through our orchard with his head lowered, hoping I'd not see him until he was close enough to pretend he'd always been right there! Sometimes I'd even see him begin to creep away from me as I worked outside.

I'd use my classroom-teacher eyes to watch him without him knowing it. He'd walk behind the nearest pine tree and lay down for a while. Then he would slowly walk to the next tree and lie down again. Oh, so innocently he'd glance back to see if I had noticed he was no longer close to me.

"Simbaaa," I'd say with a disappointed inflection in my voice. He would stand and trot back to me with such a tail-wagging sweetness that all I could do was cuddle him. Rarely did I have to scold that dear dog, but there were times when I first brought him home with me that it was necessary. He would often growl at guests, taking longer to warm up to them than I liked. I would punish him by making him sit away from me.

It was apparent the first day I brought him home that Simba might have been an over-achieving guard dog in his former home. He was very skittish and seemingly untrusting, even with Tom when they first met. I was holding Simba on a leash near what was to be his outside doghouse. He growled when Tom approached. I asked Tom to bring Simba some food, and he brought him a new bowl of food. Simba immediately realized he should love Tom, too. During Simba's first weeks with us, he nipped visitors' pants legs and held on three times. Strangely enough, each of the three people he nipped was named Mike!

The first was a twelve-year-old neighbor boy who rode his bicycle up our lane while Simba and I were in the garden. I called to Mike to stop because Simba's back had ruffed up and he gave a low growl. Mike called out, "I'm not afraid of dogs!" and continued riding toward me. Simba ran to him and sniffed his ankles before taking a soft grasp of one of them and holding on until I could get there and tell him "No!"

I made Simba sit behind me while I visited with Mike, who I scolded a bit for continuing to approach rather than stopping as I had warned him. I explained that we wanted Simba to be a good guard dog because we live far back off the main road and I felt more comfortable working outside alone when Simba was nearby. Mike promised he'd not come to visit unannounced again.

The next Mike-nipping incident was when good friends of ours came with their son to fish and boat on our pond. Simba was welcoming and well-behaved while we all visited in a group by our dock. However, when Mike walked away from us a short distance to look into the pond, Simba walked with him and held him by the cuff of his pants while looking back at me! I told him, "No!" and he immediately walked contritely to my side. Luckily, this Mike had a dog of his own and was not dismayed by Simba's guarding nature.

The third time Simba held a Mike by the leg happened inside our house. Two other couples were visiting in the evening, and we were having fun conversation seated in front of our fireplace. Our friend, another Mike, walked to the deck door to look outside across the pond.

He called to me, "Jessie, your dog has hold of my pants leg!"

I called, "Simba, no!" and he quickly released Mike's cuff. Again, Simba was contrite as he leaned into my legs and looked up at me.

Because that Mike was a bit less understanding, we put Simba in the garage for the remainder of the evening.

That was the last time he ever nipped anyone. However, we always watched him carefully when we had guests. I think maybe he'd been trained by his previous owner to nip first and look for permission later!

There was no more loyal dog than Simba. Even though he loved my husband, it was obvious that Simba was *my* dog. He followed me around the house as I did laundry or cleaned. While we were watching TV, he couldn't bear to have me out of his sight long enough for me to go to the kitchen and come right back. I'd say, "Stay here, Simba. You don't need to get up. I'll be right back." He would lift his head, watch the door for a moment after I left the room, and then would lumber to his feet and pad after me.

One of my favorite games was to try to stand up quietly (no squeaking chair or creaking knees!) and sneak from the room without disturbing Simba's seemingly deep sleep. I was never successful! We think he constantly monitored the air in the room and knew when I was no longer in it.

As Simba aged, that sense of where I was every second got a little slower, maybe taking him a full minute to miss me, but he always eventually lifted his head, looked around, and then padded through the house to find me. That slower reaction saddened me because I knew it was a forewarning of Simba's approaching old age and eventual death."

SIMBA'S DEATH

The one story about Simba that I can hardly bear to tell or write about is his death. After nine too-short years of enjoyment and fun with that wonderfully loyal dog, he was diagnosed with an inoperable malignant tumor. Our vet told us that we should enjoy him as long as we could.

For ten months after that diagnosis we loved that dear dog's presence with us. Some days, I would almost believe that maybe the diagnosis was incorrect and he wasn't ill at all. Then, within a two-week period, he became listless, be-gan having wetting accidents in the house, and rarely ate.

Our vet had told me that we'd know when Simba's quality of life was being compromised by the illness, and we should call her. I phoned the vet on a Thursday, know-ing Simba was in great pain, and she said she'd come to our house the next day. It was the most difficult time and decision, but that sweet dog made it as comfortable for us as he could. I believe he knew from my tears that our time together was coming to a close. He'd stopped padding after me around the house and spent much of his time sleep-ing.

When the vet arrived, Simba and I were sitting in one of our favorite places, the glider on our screened porch. As Dr. Arvin and her intern came into the porch, Simba stood up in his guarding position but then sat down and let them approach. I patted the seat beside me, and even though it was painful, he hoisted himself up and laid across my lap.

With tears rolling, Dr. Arvin and her assistant petted him and crooned to him about what a good dog he was. As she shaved the injection site on his foreleg, she spoke to him quietly, telling him that she'd remember him always for the fine, loyal dog he was. Simba lay across my lap watching the vet and then me out of his tired eyes. I leaned down into his face, and as he always did, Simba lifted his chin, and I kissed him on his forehead. Then while I was holding his head, looking into his beautiful, trusting eyes, Dr. Arvin gave him the injection. Within mere seconds he totally relaxed against me and was gone. Ah, my dear boy!

For several weeks I had a mental battle with myself, thinking maybe we should have kept Simba with us longer. However, I'd taken photos of him during his last days with us, and I'd look at those and see the illness and pain in his eyes and know we'd done the right thing for him at the right time. I'm thankful to have many, many photos of Simba that were taken throughout the years he was with us. They are a joy for me to see now, even those of his final days. Those photos have been a great part of my pleasure at having known that wonderful dog and my acceptance of having to live without him.

Writing about these dog meetings and reminiscing about Trixster, Cameron, and Simba has been therapeutic for me as I've tried to accept being dogless. As everyone who is living without a favorite dog knows, we will miss them forever. Will I get another dog? I certainly hope so. Tom and I take great pleasure in occasionally "dog sitting" for family, friends and neighbors. I'm waiting for a dog to find me again and become my own. I'm trusting that it will be as sweet as Trixster, as entertaining as Cameron, and as loyal as Simba.

Trixster, Cameron and Simba
(Caricature sketch by Paul Richards)

"The bond with a true dog is as lasting as the ties of this earth can ever be."

Konrad Lorenz

LaVergne, TN USA
20 November 2009
164867LV00001B/1/P